THE SOLDIER DREAMS

THE SOLDIER DREAMS

DANIEL MACIVOR

The Soldier Dreams
first published 1997 by
Scirocco Drama
An imprint of J. Gordon Shillingford Publishing Inc.
© 1997 Daniel MacIvor
Reprinted June 2012

Scirocco Drama Editor: Glenda MacFarlane
Cover design by Terry Gallagher/Doowah Design Inc.
Cover photo by Guntar Kravis
Printed and bound in Canada

We acknowledge the financial support of The Canada Council for the Arts
and the Maniotba Arts Council for our publishing program.

Library and Archives Canada Cataloguing in Publication

MacIvor, Daniel, 1962-
   The soldier dreams

A play.
ISBN 1-896239-26-9

   I. Title.

PS8575.I86S64 1997   C812'.54   C97-901004-7
PR9199.3.M3225S64 1997

J. Gordon Shillingford Publishing
P.O. Box 86, RPO Corydon Avenue, Winnipeg, MB Canada R3M 3S3

For Mark Shields

I'd rather learn from one bird how to sing
than teach ten thousand stars how not to dance
e. e. cummings

Daniel MacIvor

Daniel MacIvor was born in Cape Breton, Nova Scotia. He is the author and director of numerous award-winning theatre productions including *See Bob Run, Wild Abandon, 2-2 Tango, This Is a Play, The Soldier Dreams, You Are Here, How It Works, A Beautiful View, Communion,* and *Bingo!* From 1987 to 2007, with Sherrie Johnson, he ran da da kamera, a respected international touring company that brought his work to Australia, the UK and extensively throughout the U.S. and Canada. With long-time collaborator Daniel Brooks, he created the solo performances *House, Here Lies Henry, Monster, Cul-de-sac* and *This Is What Happens Next.* Daniel won a GLAAD Award and a Village Voice Obie Award for his play *In On It,* which was presented at PS 122 in New York. In 2006, Daniel received the Governor General's Award for Drama for his collection of plays *I Still Love You.* In 2008, he was awarded the prestigious Siminovitch Prize in Theatre.

Acknowledgements

Thanks to the people who supported the development of this play: Deanne Taylor and VideoCabaret, Sound Image Theatre, David Duclos and The Theatre Centre East and West, and Candy Burley and Canadian Stage Company. I would also like to thank the actors who participated in the workshops: Robert Persichini, Mark Shields, Guntar Kravis and Michael Sinelnikoff. Special thanks to Sarah Phillips for her keen eye.

Characters

DAVID (1) is the dying David. He is surrounded by his care team: his lover RICHARD, his younger sister JUDY, his older sister TISH, her husband SAM. DAVID is the memory David—he exists in the past with the German medical STUDENT. Note well: in the text of the play the dying David will be denoted by "DAVID (1)"—the memory David will be simply "DAVID".

Setting

In our Toronto productions DAVID (1) in his bed dominated the space; we used no other furniture at all, but I think there are many choices between realism and minimalism for the bedroom scenes.

On either side of the bed and outside the area that we defined as DAVID's "room" were two raised platforms and on each was a microphone on a stand. On these platforms the memory scenes took place. It felt right that DAVID and the STUDENT should be an unrealistic distance apart—the microphones also helped to remove the action from the bedside scenes—more memory-like or dream-like. It wasn't until the final memory "Ottawa. Apartment. Morning." that DAVID and the STUDENT played out the scene with a physical realism.

Production Credits

The Soldier Dreams was originally produced by da da kamera and premiered at Canadian Stage Company, Toronto, on March 26, 1997 with the following cast:

DAVID (1).. John McLachlin
DAVID..Daniel MacIvor
TISH ....Caroline Gillis
SAM.. Jim Allodi
JUDY.. Heather MacCrimmon
RICHARD.. Blair Williams
STUDENT...Volker Bürger
NURSE.. Carol Gillis

Directed by Daniel Brooks and Daniel MacIvor
Dramaturged by Daniel Brooks
Set and Light Design by Jan Koma'rek
Sound and Music Composed by Richard Feren
Produced by Sherrie Johnson
Assisted by Rochelle Hum

The Soldier Dreams was the winner of two 1997 Dora Mavor Moore Awards: Best Production (da da kamera) and Best Direction (Daniel Brooks and Daniel MacIvor).

A requiem plays as the audience enters.

DAVID (1) lies motionless in the bed. The light fades and the Soldier's theme plays. The STUDENT passes through the space. He pauses and looks at DAVID (1). He exits the space. Slowly DAVID's family enters the room one by one. First TISH followed by SAM then JUDY and finally RICHARD. The four stand around the bed. DAVID enters the space and addresses the audience.

DAVID: Hello I'm David. These are some people I know. My big sister Tish, her husband Sam, my little sister Judy, my lover Richard. And the guy in the bed, that's me. And if I had my way we'd all be dancing.

The music swells and DAVID exits. The NURSE enters, sits on the edge of the bed and begins working on DAVID (1). DAVID (1) groans.

SAM: Should we be here?

RICHARD: No we should be in Miami.

SAM: Right…

DAVID (1) groans.

TISH: *(To JUDY.)* What is she doing?

NURSE: I'm inserting the drip line into the catheter in his chest.

DAVID (1) groans.

TISH: Why is he making that noise?

SAM: Is he in pain or…?

TISH: Watch his arm. That's his sore arm.

SAM: Does he need a painkiller?

TISH: Is he due for another painkiller?

RICHARD: No but I am.

TISH: Pardon me? Watch his arm.

JUDY: Guys. Let's let the nurse do her job.

Silence.

DAVID (1): Ottawa.

NURSE: Ottawa?

RICHARD: Ottawa right Ottawa.

SAM: Ottawa.

JUDY: *(To NURSE.)* He's saying that a lot.

TISH: He's remembering our wedding.

RICHARD: Your wedding?

SAM: Did something special happen at our wedding?

TISH: *(A look to SAM.)*

SAM: *(To TISH.)* Sorry.

RICHARD: He's probably just delirious.

TISH: He was Sam's best man.

SAM: Yeah.

TISH: He looked so nice.

DAVID: Matchbook.

SAM: Matchbook yeah he says that a lot too. *(To NURSE.)*

What do you suppose it means?

TISH: She's not Barnaby Jones.

SAM: No I know.

NURSE: Does he smoke?

RICHARD: No.   TISH: Yes.

RICHARD: *(To TISH.)* He quit.

NURSE: That might have something to do with it. *(To JUDY.)*
             These pyjamas?

TISH: Yes?

NURSE: I think they might be giving him a rash.

TISH: What? No, that's impossible, they're a hundred
             percent cotton.

NURSE: Yes but—see how it's red here? Cotton can be a little
             rough.

JUDY: We'll change them. Thanks,

             The NURSE exits.

SAM: He's got a bit more colour today though. Than
             yesterday.

TISH: *(To JUDY.)* You checked her references?

JUDY   Yes. She's good.

TISH: Did you see the way she moved his sore arm?

SAM: Which one?   JUDY: Which arm?

TISH: I think we should look for someone else.

JUDY: I like her.

TISH: Judy, discernment has never been your strong
             point.

JUDY: *(Moves to door.)* I'm going to get David a change of
             pyjamas.

TISH: *(To JUDY.)* Are we going to deal with this nurse
             thing?

JUDY: I like the nurse.

TISH: You like her, fine take her to a movie.

JUDY: You don't have to like her she's not your nurse.

TISH: And she's not yours either.

RICHARD: Why don't we ask David what he thinks. *(Loudly.)*
             David honey? Do you like your nurse?

JUDY: Richard!   TISH: Shhh!

RICHARD: Do you think she's competent? Well it looks like
             he's not going to rise out of his coma to tell us.

             *RICHARD exits. TISH gives JUDY a look. JUDY
             exits. TISH gives SAM a look. SAM shrugs his
             shoulders. TISH exits. SAM is alone with DAVID.
             SAM approaches the bed and looks down upon the
             silent DAVID (1).*

DAVID: Ottawa.

             *Light cross fades from the bed to DAVID and the
             STUDENT.*

             The airport. A cab. Night.

STUDENT: Hello.

DAVID: Hello. You're going downtown?

             The STUDENT nods.

             I guess we'll just split the fare or whatever.

             The STUDENT gives him a strange look.

             Oh, it looks like the rain is stopping.

STUDENT: *(Offering.)* Cigarette?

DAVID: I don't think you're allowed to…um… Sure.

> *DAVID reaches out toward the student and a cigarette appears in his (DAVID's) hand. The STUDENT lights a match from a matchbook and offers to light DAVID's cigarette.*

No thanks I quit. I just like to hold it.

> *The STUDENT gives him a strange look. Pause.*

Are you from Hamburg?

STUDENT: Pardon?

DAVID: Your matchbook says…

STUDENT: Oh yes, no I'm from Berlin.

DAVID: Oh.

STUDENT: I visit Hamburg from time to time.

DAVID: Where do you live in Berlin?

STUDENT: Do you know Berlin?

DAVID: No but I… Right.

STUDENT: I live here now. For one year. I am a student.

DAVID: Oh studying…?

STUDENT: Yes.

DAVID: No I mean what do you want to be?

STUDENT: "Want to be"?

DAVID: Um… What job are you studying to obtain?

STUDENT: A doctor.

DAVID: Ahh. *(Laughs at his inadvertent joke.)* "Ahh." *(He does it again, sticking out his tongue and putting his head back, so that he will "get it".) "Ahhhh."*

> *The STUDENT gives him a strange look, smiles weakly, turns away.*

STUDENT: *(Getting it.)* Ah! "Ahhh."

DAVID: "Ahhh."

BOTH: "Ahhhhh."

> *They laugh together. A pause.*

STUDENT: It's a nice night.

DAVID: Yes it is.

STUDENT: Perhaps we could walk.

> *Pause.*

DAVID: We could walk.

BOTH: We'll walk.

> *They laugh together.*

> *Light crossfades to the bedroom. SAM and JUDY in the bedroom. SAM makes notes in a little book. JUDY holds an unlit cigarette. TISH enters.*

TISH: Did you call about that girl?

JUDY: What girl?

TISH: The nurse.

JUDY: No.

TISH: Where's the number?

JUDY: On the fridge.

TISH: What's her name?

JUDY: Nancy.

TISH: Nancy what?

JUDY: I don't know.

TISH: You don't know?

JUDY: Nancy Nurse.

TISH moves to exit.

It's after hours, there won't be anybody in the office.

TISH: All right, fine, I'll speak to her in person the next time she's in.

Pause.

(To JUDY.) When did you start smoking?

JUDY: After Mom died.

TISH: That's smart.

JUDY: Somebody's got to carry the torch.

TISH: You're not going to smoke it in here.

JUDY: Hardly.

Pause.

TISH: Do you want some Jello?

JUDY: *(Shakes head no.)*

TISH: *(To SAM.)* Do you want some Jello?

SAM: *(Groans.)* No thanks.

RICHARD enters laughing. He carries two lottery tickets.

RICHARD: What are these?

TISH: Sorry?

RICHARD: These.

TISH: Lottery tickets?

RICHARD: Lottery tickets! From your cousins! People send cards, people send flowers, people send notes or chocolates or fruit or prayers even. People do not send lottery tickets. However, your cousins do. And not to mention all the other idiots I've been—I have been on the phone all afternoon, everybody wants the story: people he used to work with, his old boss, his hairdresser, his accountant, old boyfriends—where do these people come from, the person from the corner store called! The person we sold that carpet to, the people we rented that cottage from...I don't have time for this.

                TISH stares icily at RICHARD.

                What?

TISH: You don't have time for this?

RICHARD: No I mean I...I mean... You know.

TISH: No I don't.

                TISH exits.

RICHARD: She really doesn't like me.

SAM: No no she thinks you're great.

JUDY: *(Snorts.)*

                RICHARD gives SAM a look.

SAM: Well no not 'great' but she doesn't you know despise you or anything.

RICHARD: That's good to know.

                RICHARD exits.

JUDY: "She thinks you're great"?

SAM: *(Shrugs.)*

               Blackout on JUDY and SAM.

               A spotlight up on TISH who addresses the audience.

TISH: Hello I'm Tish, David's big sister. Tish, that's
               short for Trish, which is short for Patricia. It was
               Trish until David started to talk, but he couldn't
               say Trish he could only say Tish and so it stuck
               and so it's Tish. And so...I would like to take
               this moment for David. Of course if David had
               his way we'd probably all be dancing. David
               has always been quite the dancing fool—not me
               though—I could barely work up a shimmy at
               my own wedding reception. I guess it's safe to
               say there is no 'dancing gene'. I mean, that's to
               say it doesn't run in the family. Although Judy's
               been known to shake her leg a bit. I guess when
               they were handing out rhythm I was...shopping.
               Ha ha. *(Pause.)* Anyway. Maybe if he gets a little
               better, we'll do a little samba 'round the bed. But
               what I wanted to say *(Clears her throat.)* Excuse me.
               What I wanted to do was tell a funny little story:
               When we were kids we weren't allowed to talk at
               the dinner table. Dad used to say "Digestion not
               discussion". And because we weren't allowed to
               talk at dinner it made it difficult not to—for David
               and me at least—not so much for Judy because she
               was just a baby—and anyway whatever Dad said
               was the law for her she was always Daddy's little
               girl. *(Pause.)* Anyway! We weren't allowed to talk
               at the dinner table—and then it turned out that in
               Girl Guides I learned the sign alphabet—which
               was one of the few things I managed to learn from
               Girl Guides other than don't even think of putting
               me in a beret. Just call me Big Head. Ha ha. So. I
               taught David how to sign the alphabet and then
               at dinner we were able to communicate—you
               know, very surreptitiously, just small, like this.
               Not whole phrases or sentences or whatever of

course, just…like a code which sort of deteriorated down into just mostly: W.F. Which stood for 'Who Farted.' And there were variations on that like Y.F. for 'You Farted' and H.F. for 'He Farted'—and there was also S.D.A. for 'She's Drunk Again'—ha ha, poor old Mom. But um mostly W.F.

So. Anyway.

But the thing is. The point is about the connection that David and I have. This secret little language we created back then represents—something special. Something private. Just for us. Something special that I would never be able to have with anyone else. And also of course it talks about David and what a funny—what a wonderful sense of humour he had—he has—and you know, things like that. Thank you.

> *Spot fades on TISH.*

> *Light snaps up in the bedroom. JUDY, SAM and RICHARD are there.*

SAM: And the guy—the guy leans over the table and the doctor reaches in and he pulls out a dozen roses and the doctor says to the guy, "Do you know you have a dozen roses up your butt?" And the guy says, "Read the card! Read the card!"

> *RICHARD and JUDY do not respond.*

JUDY: Um.

SAM: *(To JUDY.)* "Read the card!"

JUDY: The doctor said that?

SAM: No, the guy.

JUDY: Oh the roses were for the doctor!

SAM: From the guy!

JUDY: *(Laughing.)* Oh that's funny.

RICHARD: I don't think it's funny.

SAM: Well it's… Why not?

RICHARD: I think it's bordering on homophobic actually.

SAM: No it's…no…I… Why?

RICHARD: It's a 'gay' joke. The fact that it exists is offensive—like a 'Newfie' joke or a 'Jew' joke. The content is irrelevant.

SAM: But, well, I didn't make it up.

RICHARD: Yes but you tell it.

SAM: But, well… But the person who told me was gay.

RICHARD: Well that doesn't surprise me—homosexuals are notoriously homophobic.

SAM: Well? So? Sorry, you mean—

RICHARD: I'm not accusing you. I'm just saying we have to watch out for these insidious little things.

SAM: Uh…right.

JUDY: The thing about the joke that sort of threw me was the 'butt'.

SAM: What?

JUDY: That the doctor said "Roses up your butt". Would a doctor say 'butt'? Wouldn't a doctor say 'rectum' or something.

SAM: Yeah but—rectum's not funny.

JUDY: I think rectum's funny, I think rectum's hilarious.

RICHARD: Irregardless of the wording it's still offensive.

JUDY: Oh Richard.

TISH enters.

TISH: Where is that carpet?

RICHARD: Which carpet?

TISH: Mom's carpet that David had on the wall upstairs.

RICHARD: Oh um.

JUDY: Oh yeah, where is that carpet?

RICHARD: I'm not sure.

TISH: It's a very valuable carpet.

RICHARD: Well it's David's so...

TISH: Actually it's mine. Mom gave it to me.

JUDY: When?

TISH: Ages ago. Before Dad died.

JUDY: Oh.

TISH: I'd just like to know where it is.

RICHARD: You'll have to—I don't know—maybe in the base-
             ment.

TISH: The basement? Doesn't your basement flood?

JUDY: Oh that's not good.

TISH: It's a very valuable carpet.

RICHARD: You said that already, what are you getting at.

             Pause.

TISH: I'm not "getting at" anything—it's—I—We have
             room for it now and I thought we'd take it with us
             when we leave.

RICHARD: You're leaving?

TISH:	No—I mean—Eventually we'll be leaving.
SAM:	We don't need—we've got carpets and there's that floor painting thing you said you wanted to—
TISH:	*(To RICHARD.)* I'd just like to see it.
RICHARD:	Well I'm sorry but it has nothing to do with me okay.
TISH:	Look—
RICHARD:	Don't "look" me.
JUDY:	Guys…

The NURSE enters and sits on the bed.

NURSE:	Hello.
JUDY:	Hi.

RICHARD exits. TISH gives JUDY a look.

Excuse me.

TISH gives SAM a look.

SAM:	Um. I'll just. Excuse me.

SAM exits. TISH turns away to prepare herself to speak to the NURSE.

NURSE:	*(To DAVID (1).)* How are we doing?
TISH:	*(Turning to NURSE.)* Well actually not too good. *(Realizing the NURSE is talking to DAVID.)* I'm sorry…

The NURSE looks at TISH and then back to DAVID (1).

NURSE:	*(To DAVID (1), re: rash.)* Oh that's looking a lot better. *(Taking DAVID (1)'s hand.)* It's a beautiful night out.

TISH watches the NURSE and DAVID (1).

Light fades down to TISH and then crosses to the STUDENT and DAVID.

STUDENT:　　Beautiful.

DAVID:　　　Yes, I like this place.

STUDENT:　　You know Ottawa well.

DAVID:　　　Not really. Just a few bars, and this spot.

STUDENT:　　There are many men in this park.

DAVID:　　　Um. Well. Yeah…

　　　　　　　Pause.

My sister's getting married. Tomorrow. She lives here. In Ottawa. That's why I'm here.

STUDENT:　　That's wonderful.

DAVID:　　　Well the guy she's marrying is a bit of a geek but…

STUDENT:　　"Geek"?

DAVID:　　　Um…geek…well…

STUDENT:　　'Weird'?

DAVID:　　　Weird yeah weird.

STUDENT:　　Weird can be good.

DAVID:　　　Well yeah weird can be good. I'm the best man.

STUDENT:　　Best of what?

DAVID:　　　No for a wedding there's a…never mind.

STUDENT:　　Oh yes of course.

　　　　　　　Pause.

The water is so still.

DAVID: The lights are beautiful.

STUDENT: Yes. More so in the water. Of their reflection. This is
                the difference between a reality and a memory. The
                reflection is the memory of the light. The memory
                is always more wonderful.

DAVID: Not always.

STUDENT: Ah, now you speak from desire.

                Pause.

DAVID: I should go.

STUDENT: To a bar?

DAVID: A bar?

STUDENT: Okay.

DAVID: Oh...'kay.

                *Lights fade out on DAVID and the STUDENT and
                cross to the bedroom.*

                SAM and RICHARD stand near the bed. Silence.

SAM: "We seek certainty, not knowledge." Bertrand Rus-
                sell.

                Silence.

                You know, like they say, time is fleeting and so on,
                sometimes maybe it's better to know. For all of us
                really it's just a matter of. You know. 'Once' was
                once 'soon'.

                Silence.

                Or some people's ideas about the unendingness
                of the energy of the essence or. Which actually has
                you know scientific um, a scientific—in that energy
                cannot be created or destroyed and so on.

Silence.

Of course Tish would just say "Some things just can't be explained." "And that's probably the way it should be." Not that I. Or. Whatever.

RICHARD: *(Sigh.)* Fuck.

SAM: Yeah.

RICHARD: Can I talk to you?

SAM: Sorry?

RICHARD: I just need to talk.

SAM: Oh sure yeah. Um.

RICHARD: It's just I find it difficult to talk to Tish.

SAM: Uh huh.

RICHARD: And Judy well, she's kind of in her own world you know.

SAM: Uh huh.

RICHARD: And anyway, they're his sisters…and to talk to them about David and I and our sexual relationship…

                Pause.

SAM: Uh huh.

RICHARD: You see we weren't. *(Sigh.)* We weren't exclusively together. And we hadn't been for a long time. You know?

SAM: Uh.

RICHARD: We saw other people.

SAM: Oh right of course. No I mean not 'of course' I mean… Sorry. Go on.

RICHARD: No it's just—I mean we always saw other people, and I mean maybe that's part of the reason we've stayed together all these years, maybe it was good for the relationship, but see we never talked about it, it was just this unspoken understanding—and I wonder why didn't we talk about it—but I never wanted to talk about it—and I mean David never brought it up and I mean I think about all that and I ask myself, or try to figure out what do I really feel about that, about David, about what's happening now—and when I do that, when I really look at how I feel, I think 'Well, irregardless of everything I—'

SAM: Regardless.

RICHARD: What?

SAM: Uh. No. Uh.

RICHARD: What did you say?

SAM: Regardless. You said... Irregardless isn't a word.

            Silence.

            Regardless will do fine.

            Silence.

            The 'ir' kind of makes it a double negative.

RICHARD: A double negative.

SAM: Yeah. Sorry. Go on.

RICHARD: What?

SAM: Do you want to—go on or?

RICHARD: No that's fine.

            Silence.

SAM: Oh. Um. I'm going to—get a tea or—Do you want some?

RICHARD: No thanks.

SAM: Excuse me.

             SAM exits. Silence.

DAVID (1):   Ottawa.

RICHARD: Ottawa, yes yes yes wherever.

             Light fades on RICHARD.

             Spot fades up on SAM addressing the audience.

SAM: I um—of course I'm just an in-law here but I uh still I would like to take this moment for David—well if I were going to do something for David—I mean if David had his way we'd probably all be dancing—that's what he loved—he said it was good for the soul. Um. Yes. Um. Soul. Hm. Words. Words. Problematic. Words trap thoughts. Words are like little cages for thoughts. So you trap the thought in the cage of the word and you look at it and you think: 'Well that's not what I was looking for at all' so then you either let it go or make do, and if you do try to make do well by that time the thought's changed so much all you're really left with is the cage. Problematic. But...David and I had a special way of communicating whenever... Well not to say I knew David all that terribly well—I didn't, uh don't, never really um. I mean I met Tish and then Tish and I got married, but David was always you know travelling and you know busy and... Of course he was my best man at our wedding—but that was more Tish's thing—she wanted that—and that was, you know, fine. So, but, yes, okay. Okay. One Christmas we were visiting David, and David and I stayed up after the others went to bed to have a few—well a few more—but um and I mentioned that I could sign the alphabet—which I can because my brother had temporary hearing loss from an accident one summer—he was driving one of those—

and um right so. And I mentioned that I could sign
and David seemed very interested in that and so
I taught him how to do it—he actually caught on
you know pretty quickly. Um but it became this
thing that we had that—I mean it became our own
kind of thing—our own little code. Like this for
example: *(Makes the sign of 'B' three times.)* which is
'B, B, B,' which stands for 'blah blah blah'—which
whenever we were in a room with someone or
other who was going on and on about something
or other we would do our 'b,b,b' which was you
know funny, but also something private, something
special, something…you know…nice… and which
is interesting because it you know asks the ques-
tion I mean is this *(Gives a thumb's up.)* this a word
or a signal or a symbol or what—is a word sonic or
verbal or mental or… But anyway that's just…*(He
signs 'b,b,b'.)*. Um. Thanks. Sorry. Thanks.

> *Spot fades out on SAM.*

> *Light fades up on TISH, sitting on the bed, holding
> DAVID (1)'s hand. SAM enters, making notes in
> his book. TISH fusses with the bed and begins speak-
> ing to DAVID (1).*

TISH: You know what I'm going to do?

> *SAM looks up and sees TISH is speaking to DAVID
> (1).*

I'm going to make some Jello. For you and me and
Sam. That would be nice eh? *(To SAM.)* You'd like
some Jello wouldn't you Sam?

SAM: Hm?

TISH: Some Jello?

SAM: God no. Please no more Jello.

TISH: *(To DAVID (1).)* Then you and I will have some.

SAM: Tish I really don't think David's going to be eating any Jello.

TISH: I know it's just cheery to have around. *(To DAVID (1).)* Remember Mom's Jello? It took forever to harden because she made it with vodka. And that time we got into Mom's Jello and we got lipstick all over her mink coat? Of course it wasn't really mink—she called it mink but it was really beaver or something.

DAVID (1): Ottawa.

TISH: *(Moving away from DAVID (1).)* Ottawa. Yes that was fun wasn't it.

DAVID (1): Matchbook.

TISH: Matchbook. *(Pause.)* Oh my God!

SAM: What?

TISH: He's remembering those little matchbooks we had made up for our wedding.

SAM: Really?

TISH: Well sure.

SAM: Do you really think our wedding was that important to him?

Silence.

TISH: I guess people don't do matchbooks anymore. I wonder what they do now?

SAM: Coasters.

TISH: Coasters?

SAM: When Sidney and Sandra got married they had laminated coasters made with their pictures on them.

TISH: Really?

SAM: They're splitting up.

TISH: I heard.

SAM: Lucky we didn't do coasters.

              Pause.

TISH: What are you writing?

SAM: Nothing.

TISH: A little poem?

SAM: Notes, nothing.

DAVID (1):   German doctor.

SAM: What?

TISH: 'The German doctor', he's been saying it all morning.

              RICHARD enters.

SAM: Do you know a German doctor?

RICHARD: Oh that. I think it's just from a TV program.

SAM: Oh right, that show with the German doctor. And that actress. She's good.

RICHARD: *(To TISH.)* Um.

TISH: *(Moving to exit.)* Excuse me.

RICHARD: Listen…

TISH: What?

RICHARD: Can we call a truce here?

TISH: I don't know what you're getting at.

RICHARD: Okay, okay…

TISH: Excuse me I'm going to go make some Jello.

RICHARD: No! No more Jello! Nobody wants your fucking Jello!

TISH: Don't swear at me.

RICHARD: I'm sorry.

TISH: Who do you think you are?

SAM: All right now all righ—

Loud bass from next door pounds through the wall.

TISH: *(To RICHARD.)* What is that?

RICHARD: The guy next d— I'll deal with it.

RICHARD exits.

A quick crossfade from the bedroom to DAVID and the STUDENT. The music grows louder. They shout over the music.

DAVID: —and the Doctor says "Did you know you've got a dozen roses up your ass?" And the fag says "Read the card! Read the card!"

STUDENT: *(No laugh.)*

DAVID: "Read the card!" Get it?

STUDENT: I don't like this joke.

DAVID: Why not?

STUDENT: It makes fun of people.

DAVID: Well it's a joke, that's what it's supposed to do.

STUDENT: So I don't like jokes maybe.

DAVID: Oh come on! Lighten up.

STUDENT: No you don't understand.

DAVID: It's just for a laugh.

STUDENT: To me life is a war and it is very important what side you choose to be.

DAVID: Well even in a war they take a break from time to time.

STUDENT: Even when the soldier dreams the war goes on.

             Silence as the music continues.

DAVID: So you don't like jokes. What do you like?

STUDENT: I like to dance.

DAVID: Now you're talking!

STUDENT: But not here.

DAVID: I know a place—

STUDENT: I live nearby.

DAVID: Uhhhhhh…I don't know.

STUDENT: Because I don't like your joke?

DAVID: No…because…uh…

STUDENT: The doctor orders.

             Light snaps out on DAVID and the STUDENT.

             Light up in the bedroom. TISH, SAM and JUDY are there as the music continues. Suddenly the music cuts out. After a few moments RICHARD returns.

RICHARD: That was no problem. If it ever happens and I'm not here just knock on the door. He's very easy-going.

             Silence.

JUDY: *(To SAM.)* What are you writing?

SAM: Oh just…nothing.

JUDY: What is it?

SAM: It's a little…sort of a haiku.

JUDY: Read it.

TISH: He never reads what he writes.

JUDY: You have to.

SAM: Do I?

JUDY: It doesn't really exist if you don't share it.

RICHARD: Oh help.

JUDY: Read it.

SAM: Well…

JUDY: Read it.

SAM: *(Clears throat.)* Um. It's a nice little book isn't it.

JUDY: Read it.

                    Silence.

SAM: Um. Okay. Um. *(Reading.)* "I asked Why, Why
               answered not."

                    Pause.

               I should read it again. *(More confident.)* "I asked
               Why, Why answered not."

                    Pause.

RICHARD: That's it?

SAM: It's a haiku—

RICHARD: It's not a haiku.   TISH: No it's not.

SAM: Yeah it's—

RICHARD: *(Reaching for notebook; SAM hangs on to it.)* Let me

	see.
TISH:	No it's not.
RICHARD:	A haiku has three lines.
TISH:	And fourteen syllables.
RICHARD:	Sixteen.
TISH:	Right. Sixteen syllables.
RICHARD:	That's not a haiku.
JUDY:	Well it's haiku-like.
TISH:	It's short.
RICHARD:	*(Laughing.)* It's got that yeah, it's short.
TISH:	But so's 'Pass the salt.'
RICHARD:	'You want fries with that?'
TISH:	Good haiku!
RICHARD:	Food haiku!
TISH:	Haiku Cafe!

TISH and RICHARD laugh snortingly.

SAM:	Thanks.
JUDY:	It's nice. It's sad.
SAM:	Whatever.
JUDY:	*(Looking at the notebook.)* And you've personified 'Why'.
SAM:	Yeah right—a capital 'W'. *(To TISH and RICHARD.)* It's personification.

RICHARD and TISH continue to laugh.

JUDY:	The search for reason.

SAM: Right.

TISH: *(Laughing.)* Oh spare me.

           TISH exits.

RICHARD: *(Laughing.)* I need a drink.

           RICHARD exits.

JUDY: Guys.

           SAM and JUDY are alone. He looks down at his book. She looks at SAM. She tweaks his nipple and exits. SAM looks perplexed. Light fades on SAM.

           Light fades up in spots on TISH and RICHARD. They stand on either side of the stage, each holding a drink.

TISH: Don't get me started on Judy.

RICHARD: Don't get me started on Judy.

TISH: Angst Princess.

RICHARD: The Queen of The Hemp Parade.

TISH: Anti-socialite of the year.

RICHARD: Wouldn't want to go through customs with her, know what I mean?

TISH: You know the type.

RICHARD: And don't get me started on Sam.

TISH: And Sam…

RICHARD: A touch of the poet goes a very long way.

TISH: Poor old Sam.

RICHARD: Makes Don Knotts look smooth.

TISH: He just needs a bit of a push.

RICHARD: You know the type.

TISH/
RICHARD: And don't get me started on Her Majesty. Her Majesty!

TISH: Oh well doesn't the sun rise and set on Her Majesty.

RICHARD: Doesn't Her Majesty have to run every show.

TISH: The dramatics, really!

RICHARD: And the Jello crusade!

TISH/
RICHARD: And don't get me started on the carpet.

TISH: The carpet.

RICHARD: The carpet.

TISH: It's a very valuable carpet.

RICHARD: *(Mocking.)* "It's a very valuable carpet."

TISH: But don't get me started.

RICHARD/
TISH: And don't get me started on the wedding.

TISH: The wedding.

RICHARD: The wedding.

TISH: Okay David says to me:

RICHARD: David says to me:

TISH: David says: "About the wedding, Richard's not coming."

RICHARD: David says: "About the wedding, you're not invited." And I think:

TISH/
RICHARD: Okay. If that's the way Her Majesty wants it that's the way it's going to be.

TISH: Maybe a family means nothing what do I know.

RICHARD: Family doesn't matter to her that's fine.

TISH: But a wedding   RICHARD: But a wedding is
                   only happens   one of those
                   once—knock on   opportunities to
                   wood—and maybe   forge the family
                   fine a person   bonds—and fine a
                   doesn't believe in   person is ignorant
                   marriage that's a   and frightened of
                   person's prerogative   certain lifestyles
                   but if nothing else   but this is family
                   a little common   and that's
                   courtesy.   something else.

TISH/
RICHARD: But I guess that's my problem.

TISH: Her Majesty's problem?

RICHARD: Her Majesty's problem?

TISH/
RICHARD: A lack of compassion stemming from a basic fear
                   of intimacy.

TISH: See.

RICHARD: Simple.

TISH: You know the type.

RICHARD: But don't get me started.

TISH: And anyway…

RICHARD: this isn't about

TISH/
RICHARD: Her Majesty.

RICHARD: And

TISH: this

RICHARD:	isn't
TISH:	about
RICHARD:	me...
TISH:	*(A toast.)* To...
RICHARD:	*(A toast.)* To...
TISH:	To David.
RICHARD:	To David.

Light snaps out on TISH and RICHARD.

Light snaps up on JUDY, she addresses the audience. As she speaks she peels an orange.

JUDY: Yeah, so. Right. *(Mumbling to herself:)* Whatever whatever I don't know whatever. *(Sighs; resumes speaking normally.)* Yup. 'Kay. Good. Whatever. I would like to take this moment for David. Of course if David had his way we'd probably all be dancing. Maybe we should be, I don't know, maybe that's what should happen now. If there's such a thing as 'should'. *(Sigh.)* David's my brother and he's dying. That's all I know. That used to make me mad but not anymore, what's the point? Who am I going to be mad at? It's not your fault. Is it? *(Laughs.)* I guess it's just 'God's' fault or whatever... whoever...whatever. *(Pause.)* What am I supposed to say? It's just more talk, right. See that's something that me and David liked to do—get away from all the talk. We used to go out to clubs: Kick It, Jump, Go-Go, Smash—of course none of them exist anymore either... But uh... Yeah we used to go out and stand there in the middle of the dance floor and it would just be noise noise noise and you couldn't talk, you couldn't think, you couldn't even feel anything, except the beat—and that was so cool. And we had this way of communicating in this weird language we invented—see I taught

David how to do the sign language alphabet—I learned it from this girl this deaf girl in this welding course I took—and I taught him…well I tried to teach him but he wasn't catching on too quick… or maybe I was just a bad teacher—but we worked out this other kinda way of doing it which would be like *(Makes the sign for 'p' and points over her shoulder.)* for 'gotta pee', and *(Makes the sign for 'c', the sign for 'f' and covers her ears.)* meant 'check out the freak on the speaker', and other stuff, much more nasty, about guys and you know… *(Laughs.)* like *(Makes the sign for 'h' twice then gestures toward her pelvis.)* and I won't even tell you what that means *(Laughs.)*…Yeah, anyway…but that was our special, private, personal thing. Ours. And that was so cool. There's nobody like David. *(Pause.)* Anyway whatever that's all.

> *She throws the orange peel on the floor. She turns toward the bedroom. Lights go up suddenly on SAM sitting on the bed. She walks toward the bedroom watching SAM. Through the scene she eats her orange.*
>
> *Silence.*

JUDY: You're always hiding in here.

SAM: I like it in here. It's peaceful.

JUDY: He said anything?

SAM: "Matchbook."

JUDY: Tish said she thought it was something to do with the matchbooks from your wedding.

SAM: Oh yeah?

JUDY: I doubt that though.

SAM: Yeah. Well, who knows?

JUDY: I wonder if he just wants a cigarette.

SAM: Maybe.

JUDY: I wonder what he wants.

SAM: Maybe he doesn't want anything.

JUDY: He must want something or he wouldn't still be alive.

    Silence.

    He started going back to church.

SAM: Really.

JUDY: Mmm.

SAM: Well he's a bit of a fatalist—that's pretty Christian. He always believed in reasons for things.

JUDY: I don't.

    Silence.

SAM: Yeah, but it's probably better to believe in reasons for things than not to—don't you think?

JUDY: Why?

SAM: What have you got to lose?

JUDY: Dignity.

SAM: Well dignity's not going to do you a hell of a lot of good when you're dead.

    Silence.

JUDY: Hey. Do you wanna smoke a joint?

SAM: Oh. No. Thanks. Um. Here?

JUDY: Yeah right, Tish'd love that wouldn't she.

She hands SAM a slice of her orange and eats the last slice herself.

SAM: Yeah, really, yeah.

JUDY holds up her sticky, wet hands and walks behind SAM. She dries her hands in his hair. She pats his hair back into shape and stands behind him with her hands on his shoulders.

Silence.

JUDY: I asked Why. Why answered not.

Light crossfades from the bedroom to DAVID and the STUDENT.

DAVID: You have a cat.

STUDENT: Pardon?

DAVID: The kitty litter in the bathroom.

STUDENT: Ah yes, no. She ran away.

DAVID: Oh that's too bad.

STUDENT: This happens in life. Things go away when they must.

DAVID: Still it's sad.

Pause.

STUDENT: Will you have some music?

DAVID: Sure. What have you got?

STUDENT: Carol King or ABBA.

DAVID: What?

STUDENT: I have two CDs: Carol King or ABBA.

DAVID: Oh, well, you pick.

STUDENT: You like to be told what to do.

DAVID: *(He raises his hand to his forehead, embarrassed.)* Aaaah...

STUDENT: You have nice hands. You should speak with them.

DAVID: Speak?

STUDENT: I know the alphabet letters of hands. Shall I teach you.

               Pause.

DAVID: Sure.

STUDENT: 'A'.

DAVID: 'A'.

STUDENT: 'B'.

DAVID: 'B'.

STUDENT: 'C'.

DAVID: 'C'.

STUDENT: 'D'.

DAVID: 'D'.

STUDENT: You are a fast learner.

DAVID: I'm good with my hands.

STUDENT: Oh, so you're the best man with his hands.

               Light slowly crossfades from DAVID and the STUDENT to JUDY, RICHARD, TISH and SAM.

               The four stand in separate spots listening to the following tape-recorded scene. The tape is authentic; complete with the sounds of cutlery, people moving

> *about, and so on and continues, with only one*
> *interruption from JUDY, until the NURSE's*
> *appearance.*

GROUP
SINGING: ...Happy Birthday dear David. Happy Birthday to
              you.

> *Applause etc. on tape.*

DAVID: God I hate that song. If I have another birthday sing
              'Stormy Weather' or something.

TISH: Oh stop it.

DAVID: Hey I gotta great joke for you Sam.

SAM: Oh yeah?

DAVID: But not in mixed company.

JUDY: What's that supposed to mean?

DAVID: I was talking about Richard.

RICHARD: Ha ha—who wants cake?

JUDY: Oh man I'm stuffed.

TISH: It doesn't have nuts in it does it? Sam can't have
              nuts. Top that up would you thanks.

RICHARD: Really? Is it severe?

SAM: Sort of yeah.

TISH:	I thought you with were going to bring somebody Judy.	RICHARD:	A guy I work has that.
JUDY:	Yeah but—	SAM:	Uh huh it's, you know, common.

DAVID:	Yeah but her date didn't get out of jail in time.	RICHARD:	But he's allergic to everything Even ink— and he's a designer.
JUDY:	David .	SAM:	Whoa.
TISH:	You're kidding!	RICHARD:	But of course it's all on computer now.
JUDY:	He's sweet.		
TISH:	Jail?!	SAM:	Right right, I guess that makes it easier.
JUDY:	It's not like that.	RICHARD:	But I prefer a piece of paper—a nice piece of paper.
DAVID:	Fraud.		
TISH:	Oh my god.	SAM:	Yeah I like paper— I like a nice piece of paper.
JUDY:	He didn't do it!	RICHARD:	Yeah there's something about it eh?
TISH:	And what ever happened to that pusher you were dating?	SAM:	And I hate to say it but this recycled paper—
JUDY:	He wasn't a pusher!		
DAVID:	No, they call them dealers now Tish.	RICHARD:	No I know.
		SAM:	It's just not the same.
JUDY:	It was just grass!		

TISH: Well the last   RICHARD: Not the quality.
             I read it was still
             illegal. God, have
             some sense.

                                  SAM: Not like it
                                              used to be no.

JUDY: Oh and booze is   RICHARD: But whose fault
             legal so you don't   is that?
             have a problem.

TISH: What's that   SAM: No no exactly
             supposed to mean?   exactly.

JUDY: If the shoe fits sweetheart.

DAVID: Okay girls—

RICHARD: Is everything okay?   TISH: Don't start with
                                              me.

SAM: Hm?

JUDY: Well it's true, that's your second bottle this
             afternoon.

SAM: Hm?

DAVID: Who's counting?

TISH: I am not going to get angry today Judy.

RICHARD: Did everybody get cake?

JUDY: No you're just going to get drunk.

SAM: What?

DAVID: Boring!

RICHARD: Maybe we should move into the backyard.

TISH: Why do you always do this?

SAM: What?

JUDY: Why do you always condemn my life?

RICHARD: Did everybody   SAM: You okay?
                 get cake?

                                    TISH: She's just a brat.

DAVID: All right! Soul Train time!

RICHARD: Oh God.   TISH: No David.

DAVID: Yes! Judy put on something funky—Let's do "The
                 Bus Stop".

RICHARD: David…   TISH: I'm not dancing.

DAVID: Yes! It's my birthday and everybody does what I
                 say!

                 DAVID has a coughing fit.

JUDY: Do you want some water?

TISH: Is he okay?

RICHARD: Get him some water.

SAM: Um.

RICHARD: Sit up, sit up.

JUDY: Richard?

SAM: Watch his cake.

RICHARD: Thanks. Here.

                 DAVID stops coughing.

DAVID: I didn't need that lung anyway.

                 TISH exits the listening area.

TISH: Are you okay?

                 DAVID breathes with difficulty for a few moments.

DAVID: Judy?

                JUDY responds from the listening area.

JUDY: (*Aloud.*) Yeah? (*On tape.*) Yeah?

DAVID: "The Bus Stop".

TISH: Oh god.

SAM: Sorry, is this a dance thing?

RICHARD: You don't know "The Bus Stop"?

                Disco music starts.

DAVID: All right we're all going to dance—help me up—
                and then we're all going to get remarkably drunk
                and then we're all going to fight some more and
                then later I might even smoke a cigarette!

                RICHARD leaves the listening area.

RICHARD: No!

DAVID: YES! Because it's my fucking birthday!

TISH: David.

DAVID: Give it up for me sister!

                JUDY leaves the listening area.

TISH: (*Squeals.*)

SAM: Hey is this thing on?

                Tape stops.

                *Light snaps from the listening area to the bedroom.
                TISH stands near the bed watching the NURSE
                remove the tubing from DAVID (1)'s catheter.*

TISH: Is—   RICHARD: Has—

RICHARD: Has he said anything?

NURSE: No.

The NURSE exits.

RICHARD: Yesterday he kept talking about the squeaky bed?

TISH: This bed?

RICHARD: I don't think the bed squeaks.

TISH: I've never heard it squeak.

RICHARD: It's a shitty old bed.

TISH: He's had it forever.

RICHARD: I wanted to get a proper bed. You know, a hospital bed.

TISH: Right right.

RICHARD: He made me promise I'd keep this one.

Pause.

TISH: It's a shitty old bed but I don't think it squeaks.

RICHARD: He doesn't move enough to make it squeak.

TISH: No I guess not.

Pause.

RICHARD: But when she sat down before I thought it might have squeaked.

TISH: Or maybe it's the floor.

RICHARD: Oh yeah the floor is terribly squeaky.

TISH: Maybe that's it.

The NURSE re-enters.

It might be the floor that's squeaking.

NURSE: Okay now—

TISH: But if it's the bed it would be easy enough to fix. Excuse me.

                TISH exits.

NURSE: Okay now, you see how his breathing's gotten very shallow?

RICHARD: Right.

NURSE: And remember how I said before—

RICHARD: Right.

NURSE: So if there are any final preparations—

RICHARD: Okay right.

NURSE: —then now would be the time.

RICHARD: Okay yes.

NURSE: If there's anything I can do...

RICHARD: Okay. Thank you. Right.

                The NURSE exits. RICHARD signs the letter 'Y', the letter 'O', the letter 'U', and then points to DAVID (1). The light fades to a low level. RICHARD sits on the bed beside DAVID (1).

                Light fades up on TISH addressing the audience. As TISH speaks JUDY enters and takes up a position at the bed. SAM enters and takes up a position.

TISH: I would like to take this moment...and I know I've already had a moment but I don't think there's a limit...ha ha. I was going to have a little slide show but I didn't really get it together to get it together. Ha ha. So, I'm um just um going to um talk you through it. Okay first there would have been a slide of—probably there would have been a screen or something here of course—and um the first slide would be David in the tub—as a baby—

a year or two old or something. And he's smiling
and there are bubbles everywhere and everything
and he's smiling. So cute. Um then um one of David and me—and that would be around David's
first day of school—and you'd see what a little
tubby I was—you'd never know it from looking
at me now—well depending on where you were
looking ha ha. And then—the next picture would
be our house and then the big backyard where we
used to play with the lake at the bottom—David
called it a lake but it was really a fish pond or
something—then—one of Mom and Dad—Dad's
got his sour face on of course and that silly hat he
always wore you can't really see his eyes there
but his eyes were really lovely—they didn't match
the frown at all—and Mom of course a little tipsy
but she was happy she was always pretty much
happy—more or less—unless she wasn't tipsy—
then she wasn't very happy at all. Ha ha. And then
a few Christmases and birthdays and so on ha ha.
Then David on his way to his junior prom with his
girlfriend Janet—they were together all through
high school—she turned out as it happens to be
a lesbian, but you'd never know it to look at her
there ha ha. Then David's trip to Greece with Judy.
That was in 1985—I know that because he's wear-
ing the sweater I gave him when he graduated
from college the year before. And um a couple
of Judy. Pictures of David sort of thin out around
here because after college he decided he didn't like
pictures—he said he wanted to remember things
just as they were in his memory.

Silence.

And of course our wedding, quite the big to-do as
you can see. David's got his nice suit on—he looks
a little tired in this picture—well we all do, that's
what weddings are like I guess.

Silence.

This isn't working. What I'll do is—I've got the slides in my suitcase and tomorrow I'll make a couple of calls—I'm sure somebody knows somebody who has a whatchmacallit to actually do it properly. So yes that would be good yes—so tomorrow. Yes.

TISH exits. Light fades up in the bedroom. After a few moments TISH enters.

Silence.

JUDY: *(Clears her throat.)*

Silence.

It's my carpet.

TISH: What?

JUDY: Mom gave me that carpet.

TISH: Well…I'm not lying.

JUDY: No I know…I just had to say that.

TISH: Well, have it, I don't care.

RICHARD: Was she drunk?

JUDY: What?

RICHARD: When she gave you the carpet—was she drunk?

JUDY: Yeah.   TISH: Probably.

RICHARD: And she was probably drunk when she gave it to David.

Silence.

JUDY: Poor old Mom.

TISH: Really Judy, you can have it.

JUDY: No forget it I'm sorry I said anything.

TISH: I'm serious, have it.

JUDY: I don't want it.

RICHARD: Look, there's no carpet. He sold it.

            Pause.

            Got ten thousand dollars for it.

            Pause.

            He went to Europe and spent the whole thing in two weeks.

            Silence.

SAM: Whoa.

RICHARD: And he didn't even take me.

            Pause.

SAM: I hope he took some pictures.

TISH: David? No.

RICHARD: He hated cameras.

TISH: He never took pictures. Not for years.

            Pause.

JUDY: I didn't know that.

            Silence. The lights shift. A spot on the STUDENT as he enters the space. He watches for someone else to appear on the other side. The four see him from the bedroom.

TISH: Who are you?

STUDENT: Hello.

TISH: What are you doing here?

STUDENT: Hello.

TISH: *(To JUDY.)* Is he a friend of yours?

JUDY: I don't think so.

TISH: Who are you?

STUDENT: I'm a friend of David's.

TISH: What accent is that?

SAM: Who is he?

JUDY: Hello.

STUDENT: Hello.

SAM: Who are you?

TISH: He says he's a friend of David's.

SAM: *(To RICHARD.)* Do you know him?

RICHARD: No.

TISH: Are you French?

RICHARD: Who is he?

TISH: He says he's a friend of David's.

STUDENT: Yes a friend of David's.

JUDY: Are you German? I think he's German.

SAM: Are you German?

STUDENT: Yes I am from Germany.

JUDY: Did you come all this way?

TISH: How do we know he's telling the truth?

JUDY: Why would he lie?

RICHARD: What's he doing here?

TISH: Ask him something German.

SAM: Uh... What... What's the capital of Germany?

STUDENT: Berlin.

SAM: *(To TISH.)* Is that right?

RICHARD: How do you know David?

TISH: Say something in German.

STUDENT: What?

TISH: Speak German.

STUDENT: Warum ist die Bananas krumm?

SAM: What did he say?

RICHARD: How do you know David?

TISH: Are you a doctor?

JUDY: Does he want to see David?

RICHARD: How do you know David?

TISH: Are you a doctor?

STUDENT: I am nothing.

TISH: Nothing?

STUDENT: I am dead.

DAVID: What's it like?

> *The four turn their attention to DAVID (1) in the bed. The light in the bedroom fades to black.*

> *A spot comes up on DAVID. DAVID faces the STUDENT from across the space.*

What's it like?

STUDENT: To be dead?

DAVID: Yes.

STUDENT: Come and see.

DAVID: No, tell me.

STUDENT: Yes. It is more beautiful than anything you can imagine. It is as if you are the emotion you feel. If you were to love a mountain or an ocean or these things, and the feeling you have in your life when you look at these things? It is as if you are that emotion. You hear a song but not only hearing it but to feel and see and smell it. The notes fly about like soft birds and in other ways it touches your tongue and fills your belly like a wonderful meal. No fear, no worry, not even ideas of these feelings. No more living between 'was' and 'will be'.

DAVID: *(Sigh.)*

STUDENT: And this idea of losing life? Don't be afraid. This is not true. Instead we have our lives back to live again—we begin over but with every answer so we can make it as we wish. Every moment perfect.

DAVID: Really?

             The STUDENT does not respond.

             Really?

             DAVID walks toward the STUDENT.

STUDENT: Ottawa. Apartment. Morning.

             DAVID stands beside the STUDENT. Light shift.

             Good morning.

DAVID: Hello.

             A cat mews.

The cat came back.

STUDENT: Yes. She had her holiday and now she's come home. Back to normal.

Silence.

DAVID: Your bed squeaks.

STUDENT: So do you.

DAVID: What?

STUDENT: What is "squeaks"?

DAVID: It makes noise.

STUDENT: So do you.

DAVID: Oh.

STUDENT: Will you have breakfast?

DAVID: Breakfast? Ah, no I don't eat breakfast.

STUDENT: Breakfast is the most important meal.

DAVID: Anyway, look I should go.

The STUDENT holds up a matchbook for DAVID. DAVID takes it.

A matchbook?

STUDENT: My telephone is inside. Should you ever need a break from the war.

Silence.

DAVID: Um. Thanks.

STUDENT: You are the best, man.

DAVID laughs. The STUDENT salutes him. DAVID laughs and gives an exaggerated salute. He turns to leave. The STUDENT disappears.

Light up on the bedroom. There is no one in the room. DAVID turns and watches as TISH and JUDY enter and remove the bedding. SAM and RICHARD enter and remove the mattress. The four return and disassemble the bed, removing it from the room. Everything is removed from the room. DAVID steps into the room. TISH enters and stands near him. She looks at the empty room. She breaks down sobbing quietly. JUDY enters. JUDY looks at TISH but cannot comfort her. JUDY exits. After a moment SAM enters. SAM puts his arm around TISH and leads her out as DAVID watches. RICHARD enters and stands near DAVID. DAVID steps toward RICHARD but stops. RICHARD takes a deep breath and approaches the audience. DAVID is still as he watches RICHARD.

A spot on RICHARD as he addresses the audience.

RICHARD: I would like to take this moment for David…

Silence.

(Clears his throat.)

Silence.

Um.

Silence.

Of course if David had his way we'd all be dancing.

RICHARD exits. The music slowly begins to swell. As the music reaches a crescendo DAVID begins to spin. DAVID falls. The music continues wildly. DAVID spins again. He falls. He tries to keep spinning. The STUDENT enters the space walking back through it in the opposite direction than he did in the beginning. The STUDENT watches DAVID. DAVID is not aware of the STUDENT but his presence gives him strength. DAVID spins wildly, and spins and spins until it is as if he flies into the air and disappears. The lights to black. The music ends.

Silence.

The End